# Ilyushin Il-2
## Viktor Povinsky
## Camouflage and markings

At the beginning of 1941, a series of new paints was approved. However, these paints were gloss, thus not accepted by VVS. Therefore, matt additives were introduced, and nitrocellulose paints emerged. Their designation consisted of the prefix "AMT" and a numeric code. The semi-matt AMT paints were intended for wooden, plywood and canvas surfaces. For metal surfaces, a series of matt oil enamels of corresponding tones was developed. Designation of the oil enamels consisted of prefix "A", numeric code and suffix "m"; Soviet documents refer also to the prefix "AM" or "FM" plus numeric code. The AMT paints could be applied either by brush, with sharp transition between colours, or by airbrush with soft transition.

### Pre-war camouflage

According to the specification issued in November 1940, the Il-2 camouflage consisted of light green A-19f on upper surfaces and light blue A-18f on undersides.

### Pre-war markings

The marking consisted of red stars with thin black outline on six positions: fuselage sides, wing upper and lower surfaces. A tactical number, usually in white, was applied on the rudder.

### 1941–42 camouflage

In June 1941, a modification of previously applied camouflage was ordered. The green upper surfaces were to be completed with patches of black. The undersides remained in light blue. In July 1941, the green AMT-4/A-24m and black AMT-6/A-28m were introduced as well as the light blue AMT-7/A-26m in August. Although the AMT paints were intended for wooden, plywood and canvas surfaces, they were applied also on the metal surfaces of the mixed construction aircraft. In this case, a special primer was used. At the same time, a camouflage consisting of green AMT-4, black AMT-6 and light blue AMT-7 was approved as the standard scheme. In the very beginning, the front line units used to improvise and apply various splotches or waves of black and green. No standard pattern was designated. However, existing photographic evidence shows aircraft with various more or less common 'unofficial' schemes. Factory No.18 used to apply a typical camouflage on some aircraft. This pattern can be easily recognized due to the large spots of black on the vertical tail. The modification of this 'basic' pattern can be seen on a few planes as well. Moreover, several Il-2s had the fighter-style camouflage applied.

In the winter period, the temporary white MK-7 was applied. It was developed in October 1941 and based on chalk and casein glue. If the recommended application technique had been followed, the original camouflage slightly showed through. This time-consuming procedure, however, was rare in combat conditions. In practice, various types of patches or waves were applied instead of the specified overall camouflage.

### 1942–43 camouflage

The first production two-seat Il-2s were camouflaged in the same way as the single-seaters: green AMT-4 and black AMT-6 on the upper surfaces and light blue AMT-7 on the undersides. In February 1943, a new camouflage was requested. It should consist of at least three tones for upper surfaces: green AMT-4, black AMT-6 and "sand" AMT-1; with undersides in light blue AMT-7. However, in April 1943, a combination of green, black and light blue was approved as a standard camouflage, which was being applied by mid summer.

### 1941–43 markings

According to the order issued in June 1941, red stars were applied on the wing undersides, fuselage sides and tail. Factory No.18 applied red stars with thin white outlines. Other factories applied red stars only. Their size and position was not specified. On the pre-war built aircraft, the wing upper surface stars should have been over-painted. The fuselage stars used to be enlarged as well as the tail stars added, usually free-hand. Tactical numbers of various shapes and colours were applied on rudder, tail fin or fuselage sides. Several regiments used to apply various stripes or bands as well as paint the propeller spinner in various colours. Diverse inscriptions completed the individual marking on several aircraft. Patriotic slogans, donator dedications or calls for revenge could be applied on one (typical for free-hand application) or both fuselage sides (if a template was used).

### 1943 standard camouflage

The order issued in July 1943 specified the standard camouflage colours as well as new standard camouflage patterns. New Il-2 camouflage of two optional patterns consisted of four colours: green AMT-4, light brown AMT-1, dark grey AMT-12 for upper surfaces and light blue AMT-7 for undersides. Both AMT-4 and AMT-7 were used before as well as black AMT-6, which was not mentioned. The light brown AMT-1 was developed in 1941 along with AMT-4 and AMT-6. However, until July 1943, it was not used. This paint could be described as light grey brown or "coffee with milk", with lots of milk. The new camouflage should have been applied from August 1943. Until then, on new production Il-2s the black AMT-6 should have been replaced by dark grey AMT-12 in the standard green – black – light blue colouring. Until the delivery of the AMT-12, the dark grey colour was made by mixing the light blue AMT-7 with black AMT-6. According to the order from July, each regiment had to have aircraft of both camouflage patterns. The "older" Il-2s with three-tone camouflage should have been over-painted only during overhauls.

As mentioned, the black AMT-6 was not included in the new camouflage order. The reason was that in the new scheme it was replaced by dark grey AMT-12. It was found that pure black is very rare on the ground and even the shadows look dark grey from higher altitudes. Therefore, black was used on propeller blades only.

## 1945 standard camouflage

In September 1943, a proposal was made to finish all VVS aircraft in the blue grey – dark grey – light blue scheme based on the current fighter camouflage. In October 1943, Ilyushin referred to the poor quality of the chalk-based white temporary paint. It was rough and worsened the aerodynamic characteristics. During combat service it often used to peel, became even rougher and dirty. In addition, its removal using warm water damaged the wooden surface. According to Ilyushin, the white paint "killed" all the efforts to improve the Il-2 quality and flight characteristics. Nonetheless, the chalk-based white was considered to be satisfactory for ground attack planes. Once again, Ilyushin proposed to introduce the "greyish" fighter camouflage, which did not required application of white in winter. The poor quality of the chalk-based white was a reason why the winter temporary camouflage was less and less common.

The order from October 1944 specified a unified camouflage scheme for all VVS aircraft as well as new camouflage patterns. The new scheme consisted of blue grey AMT-11/A-33m and dark grey AMT-12/A-32m on upper surfaces and light blue AMT-7/A-28m on undersides. Applying the temporary white in winter was cancelled. This time, only one pattern was issued for both the Il-2 and Il-10. The new camouflage should have been applied from November 1944, full transition completed in January 1945. Actually, all aircraft built in 1944 – mid 1945 wore the standard 1943 scheme. Il-2s with new camouflage were not delivered to the regiments before the war was over. Furthermore, the application of this camouflage on the Il-2 is controversial. The new "greyish" camouflage was suitable for fighters at higher altitudes. Nevertheless, it was not considered to be useful for the low-level ground attack planes. Far more effective was a camouflage including green.

## 1943–45 markings

Instruction issued in September 1943 specified for all VVS aircraft red stars with two outlines: 50mm white and 10mm red. Several aircraft carried red stars modified to "Kremlin" standard. It is not clear whether this practise related to Guard units and airmen awarded the title Hero of the Soviet Union, as sometimes stated. Smaller red stars, with or without white outline, used to be applied on propeller spinners or main landing gear nacelle tips. In several cases, the small red stars represented aerial victories achieved by gunner or pilot. Tactical numbers were applied on rudder, tail fin or fuselage sides, even on both tail and fuselage. Various identification bands, stripes or other geometric figures became more common than in 1941–43. Guards units or awarded airmen usually placed the emblems on the nose or sliding canopy. Individual marking was often completed with various inscriptions or drawings, sometimes very elaborate.

## Post-war camouflage

In the post-war period, the need for new camouflage was not so urgent. Aircraft production decreased as well. Later, the simple two-tone camouflage consisting of dark green on upper surfaces and light blue on undersides became typical for post-war piston engine aircraft.

1

## Il-2 "white 6", 504th ShAP (74th GShAP from 18th March 1943).

### Stalingrad, December 1942, pilot Snr. Lt. A. I. Borodin.

He was awarded the title Hero of the Soviet Union for his part in combat over the river Volga in 1942–43. Aircraft features late metal wings with VYa-23 and eight rocket rails mounted. The VV-1 gun-sight is installed. Sliding canopy is of late type. Winter temporary white roughly applied on the upper surfaces in green AMT-4 and black AMT-6. Only nose remained unpainted. Undersides in light blue AMT-7. Marking consists of red stars and white tactical number. Note that the tail star was applied in half on tail fin only (replacement rudder?).

2

## Il-2 "green 5".

### Unknown unit and location.

Rear fuselage section and wings of wooden construction. VYa-23 or ShVAK guns mounted. VV-1 gun-sight installed. Sliding canopy of late type. Winter temporary white partially applied on the standard two-tone upper surfaces camouflage. Undersides in light blue AMT-7. Marking consists of red stars, white tail fin leading edge and tactical number applied in interesting way.

3

Il-2 “green 5”.

4

## Il-2 "red 5".

### Unknown unit and location, summer 1942.

Aircraft built in Factory No.18 with metal wings, VYa-23 guns mounted, wooden rear fuselage section and late type canopy. Behind the cockpit, a gunner's position was installed. Factory No.18 camouflage pattern is applied. Marking consists of red stars with white outlines, red tactical number on the rudder and yellow tail tip.

5

## Il-2 “black 6”.

### Unknown unit, Moscow area, winter 1941–42.

This late Factory No.18 production aircraft is equipped with retractable ski landing gear. VYa-23 guns mounted. PBP-1b gun-sight most likely removed. Winter temporary white applied on upper surfaces, undersides in light blue AMT-7. Marking consists of red stars with black outlines and black tactical number on the rudder.

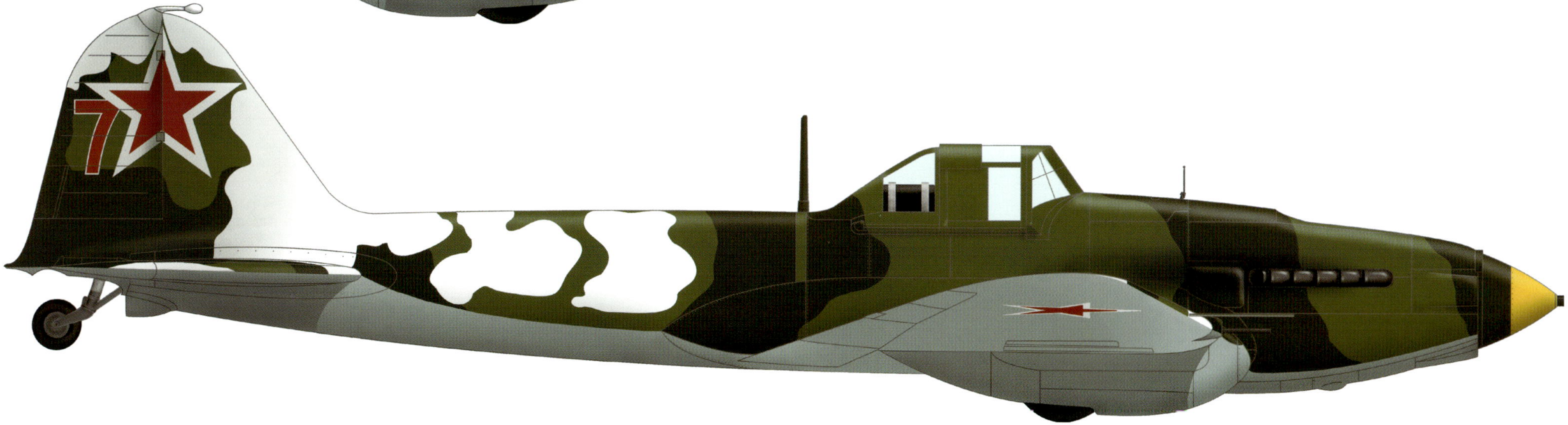

## Il-2 "red 7".

### Unknown unit, Leningrad, winter 1943.

Wings and rear fuselage section of wooden construction. ShVAK guns mounted and VV-1 gun-sight installed. Nice example of how the winter temporary camoulfage was applied in combat conditions. Upper surfaces in green AMT-4 and black AMT-6. Undersides in light blue AMT-7. Marking consists of red stars with white outlines and red tactical number of the same colours. Note the white outlines, applied also on the wing stars, were added later partially overlapping the tactical number. Fuselage stars are lacking.

Il-2 “red 7”.

## Il-2 “white 4”.

### Unknown unit and location, probably late 1941.

Built in the Factory No. 381, this early production aircraft had the metal rear fuselage section, metal wings with guns in the early configuration and the canopy of early type. “Fighter style” camouflage pattern was applied. The original rudder was replaced with one taken from another aircraft.

9

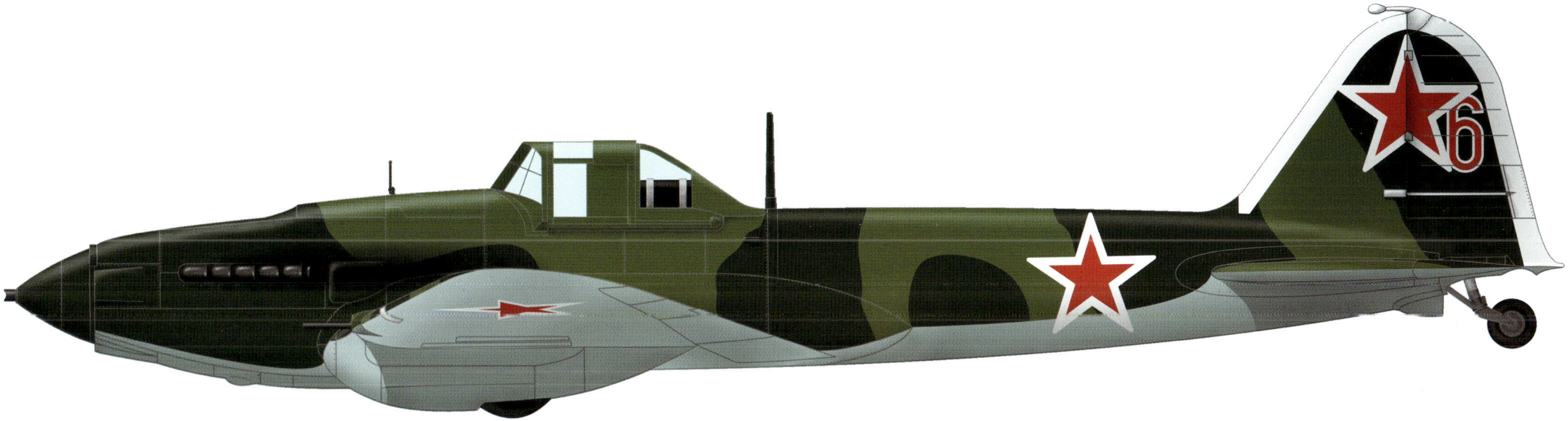

## Il-2 "red 6".

### Unknown unit and location, probably late 1943.

This aircraft was built in the Factory No.30, most likely in late 1942. VYa-23 guns have been replaced with ShVAKs. Wings and rear fuselage section of wooden construction. Typical for the Factory No.30, the "fighter style" camouflage pattern was applied. Corresponding to the new marking instructions issued in 1943, earlier aircraft could have additional white outline added to the existing red stars. Sometimes the tactical number has been partially over-painted. The "red 6" is such an example.

## Il-2 “white 6”.

### Unknown unit and location, probably late 1942.

This aircraft is a typical example of the Factory No.1 early production. Note the four-pipe exhausts. ShVAK guns in the wooden wings, the rear fuselage section is wooden as well. Upper surfaces painted in combination of green AMT-4 and black AMT-6, lower surfaces in light blue AMT-7. Plain red stars on six positions and the tactical number applied on the rudder.

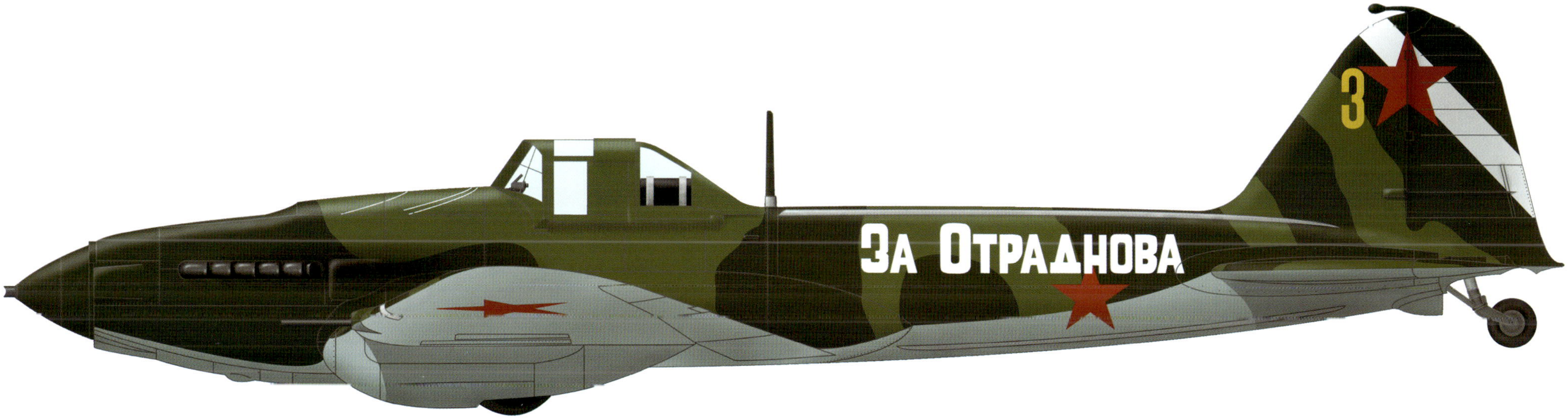


## Il-2 "yellow 3", 606th ShAP, 214th ShAD.

### Western front, October 1942. Flown by A. V. Chuvikov.

This aircraft was built before June 1942, therefore the external reinforcing ribs were added to the wooden rear fuselage section. VYa-23 guns are mounted in the wooden wings. Aircraft shows a slightly changed fighter style camouflage pattern. Marking consists of red stars, yellow tactical number on the tail fin, white diagonal stripe on the tail as well as a large inscription in white, which reads "For Otradnov". Otradnov was a regiment pilot killed in action. Note the reinforcing ribs and antenna mast holder left in bare metal.

## Il-2 "red 2", 210th ShAP.

### Southern front, March 1942. Pilot Maj. N. S. Zub.

He was awarded the Hero of the Soviet Union in memoriam after being KIA over the German Blue line in Donbas area on 22nd July 1943. Zub completed all his 382 sorties in two years of constant fighting. He was famous due to his accuracy while attacking enemy troops and equipment. The aircraft is most likely of late Factory No. 381 production. Early metal wings and wooden rear fuselage sections are fitted. Early canopy with additional armour on both sliding canopy and rear section installed. PBP-1b gun-sight removed. The overall winter temporary camouflage is typical especially for the first winter. Marking consists of red stars and red tactical number on the rudder. Huge black inscription "SMERT FASHISTSKIM OKKUPANTAM!" was applied on the fuselage. It reads "Death to fascist occupants!".

13

## Il-2 "red 21", 566th ShAP.

### Kursk area, July – August 1943.

Aircraft built in the Factory No.30, early production batches. Armed with 20mm ShVAK guns mounted in wooden wings. The landing light was of oval shape as typical for this factory. Two-seat Il-2s produced in the Factory No.30 kept wearing the typical "fighter style" camouflage, though a bit modified on this aircraft. Marking consists of plain red stars and red tactical number.

14

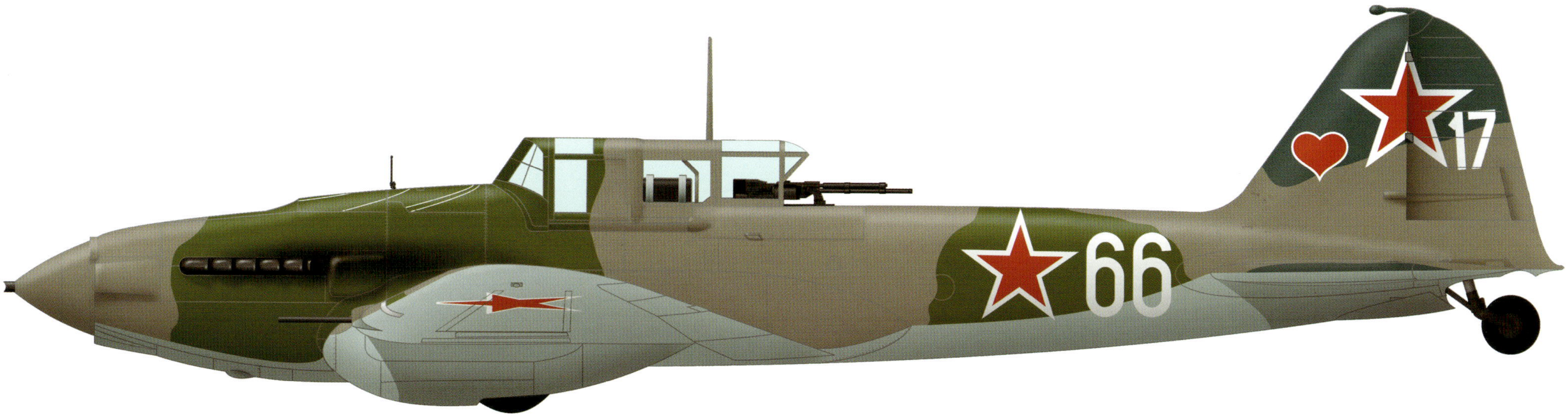

## Il-2 "white 66 – 17", 281st ShAD.

### Estonia, late 1944.

A modernized two-seater built in the Factory No.1. Note the enlarged tail wheel fairing typical for this factory, modified canopy, enlarged antenna mast and VYa-23 guns. The photograph clearly shows reinforcing belts on the wooden wings. One of the two standard camouflage patterns ordered in 1943 has been applied. The red heart seems to be the pilot's personal emblem. Two different tactical numbers are rather unusual and may indicate the aircraft was transferred from another unit.

# Il-2 "white 11", 281st ShAD.

## Estonia, late 1944.

Aircraft similar to the "white 66 – 17". It differs in other of two standard camouflage patterns applied. This is a nice example of the practice when aircraft sporting both standard camouflage patterns served in the same regiment. "White 11" had its tactical number applied on the rudder, what confirms the assumption that the "white 66 – 17" has been transferred from a unit that used to apply tactical numbers on fuselages.

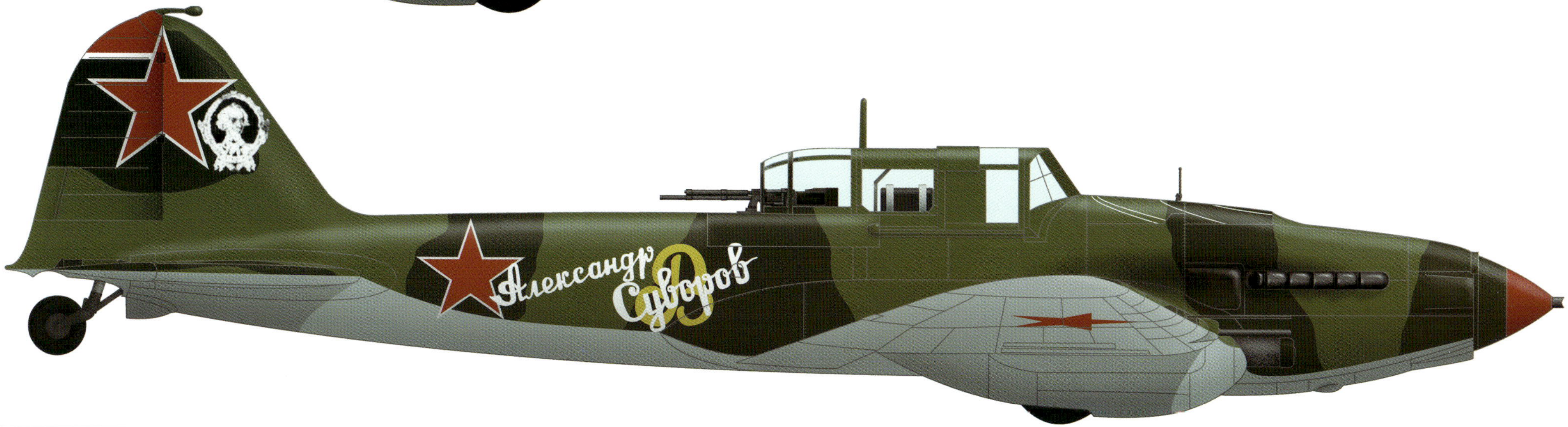


Il-2 “Alexander Suvorov”, 617$^{th}$ ShAP (167$^{th}$ GShAP from 5$^{th}$ February 1944), 291$^{st}$ ShAD, 2$^{nd}$ VA.
Kharkov front, August 1943. Pilot Jnr. Lt. V. P. Aleksukhin, gunner A. D. Gatayunov.

This crew as well as the whole regiment achieved great success in the Battle of Kursk. This aircraft was built in Factory No.18. Upper surfaces in green AMT-4 and black AMT-6. Undersides in ligh blue AMT-7. Marking consists of red stars with white outlines, red rudder tip with thin white line, white inscription “Alexander Suvorov” applied over the yellow letter “V” on the fuselage and black and white portrait of A. V. Suvorov. Propeller spinner tip painted in red.

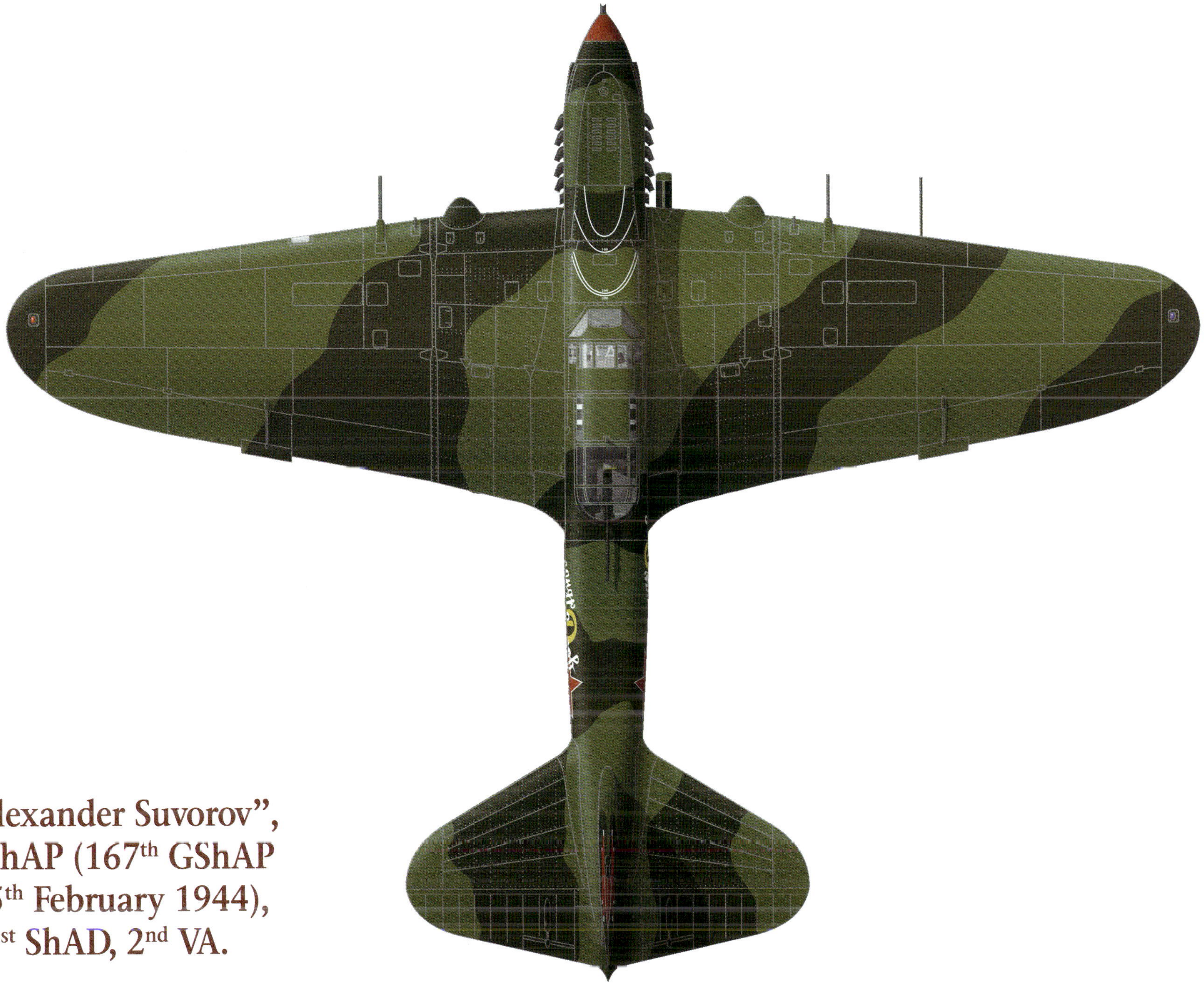

Il-2 "Alexander Suvorov", 617th ShAP (167th GShAP from 5th February 1944), 291st ShAD, 2nd VA.

## Il-2 “YAROSLAVSKIY KOMSOMOLETS”, 667th ShAP, 292nd ShAD, 1st ShAK.

### Kalinin front, January 1943.

Aircraft of this regiment were built in Factory No.30 and later purchased by members of Yaroslavl Komsomol. Wings of wooden construction with ShVAK guns mounted. Winter temporary white applied on the upper surfaces in green AMT-4 and black AMT-6. Undersides in light blue AMT-7. In this case, it is evident that the application of the white MK-7 paint did not follow the recommended instructions. Marking consists of red stars and red inscription on the fuselage.

# Il-2 "PRIVET POSLANTSAM TUVINSKOGO NARODA!".

## Unknown unit and location.

Wings of wooden construction with ShVAK guns mounted. Canopy of early type. Winter temporary white applied on upper surfaces in green AMT-4 and black AMT-6. Undersides in light blue AMT-7. Poor quality of the white MK-7 paint is well recognizable. The white is peeling and becomes rough. Marking consists of red stars and red inscription which reads "Salute to the representatives of the Tuvinsk nation!". Tactical number, if applied, is unknown.

## Il-2 “red 5”.

### Unknown unit and location.

Wings of wooden construction with ShVAK guns mounted. Canopy of early type. Winter temporary white applied only partially on upper surfaces in green AMT-4 and black AMT-6. Undersides in light blue AMT-7. Marking consists of red stars and red tactical number on the rudder.

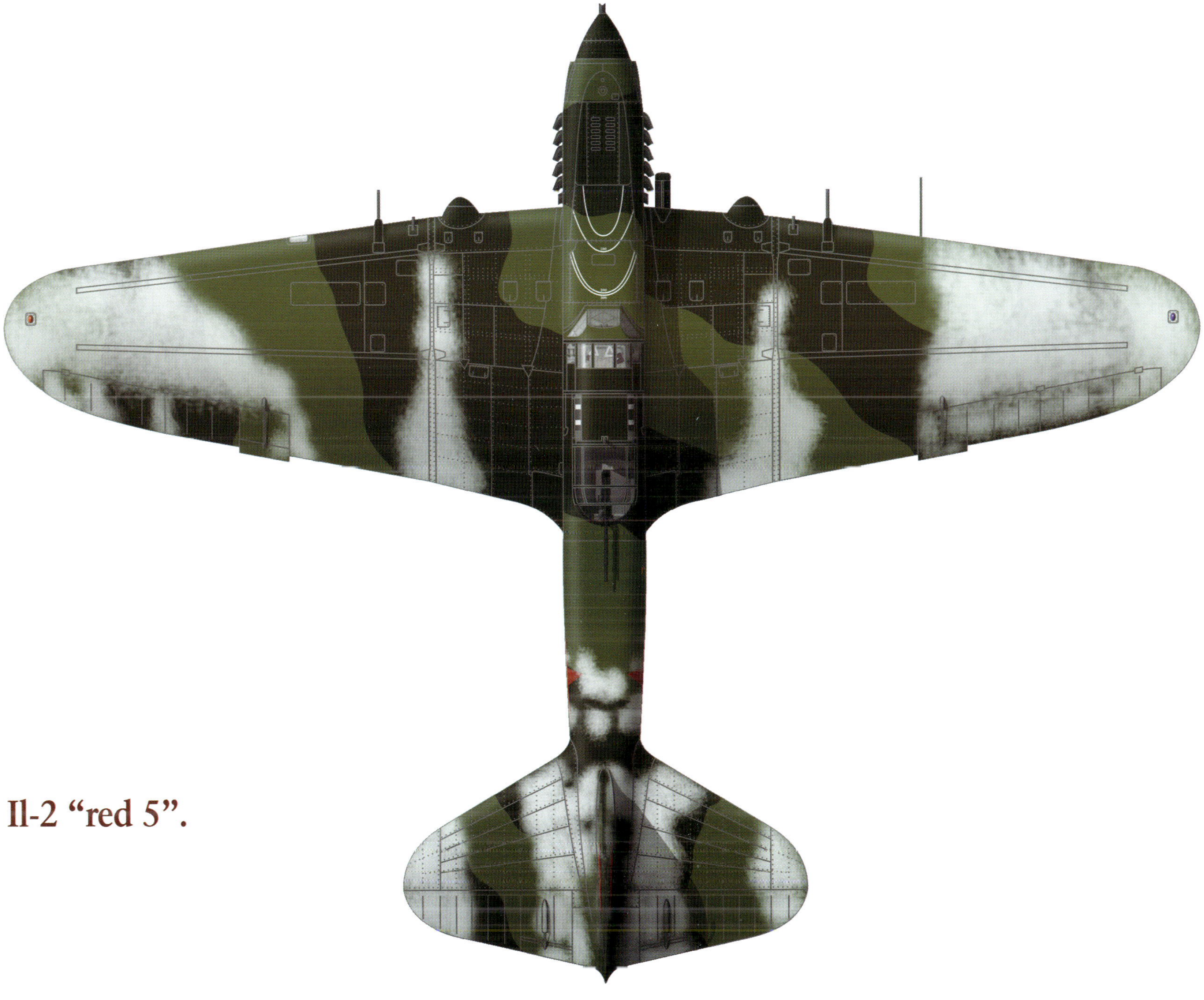

Il-2 “red 5”.

## Il-2 “white 28”, 6th GShAP.

### 1st Baltic Front, August 1944.

During the East Prussia operation, based nearby Radvilishkis, the regiment effectively engaged enemy targets in towns of Autse, Kruopyay, Yuzefovo, Kelme and Shaulyay. The pontoon bridge on the Venta River was destroyed. Il-2s of the 6th GShAP also crushed a large amount of enemy Panzers and vehicles that broke through the Shaulyay – Kelme road. An outstanding success was achieved during one sortie, when covered by Yak-3 fighters, eight Ju 87 bombers escorted by four Fw-190 fighters were intercepted. Stukas were slaughtered, just one survived. One Fw-190 was shot down as well. Il-2 crews claimed three destroyed bombers. This late production aircraft has several aerodynamics improvements implemented including modified canopy, enlarged antenna mast and repositioned pitot tube. Standard 1943 camouflage pattern applied. Marking consists of Kremlin style red stars with white and red outlines and white tactical number on the rudder.

# Il-2 "white 17", unknown unit.

## Leningrad front, May 1944.

On this aircraft, several aerodynamics improvements were applied, included modified canopy, enlarged antenna mast, repositioned pitot tube. Wings of wooden construction with VYa-23 guns mounted. Standard 1943 camouflage pattern applied. Marking consists of red stars with white and red outlines and white tactical number on both tail fin and fuselage. Note the white outlines of the fuselage and tail stars are not of same thickness.

## Il-2, "white 1", probably 810$^{th}$ ShAP.
### Flown by lt. I. I. Andreev.

Some sources place this aircraft in the city of Mtsensk area, which may indicate the period of the battle of Kursk in summer 1943. Accordingly, the "white 1" was a modernized two-seat Il-2 rather than an Il-2 with swept wings. Standard camouflage pattern applied. White tactical number and identification stripe on the tail fin. Small red stars were painted on the main landing gear nacelle tips.

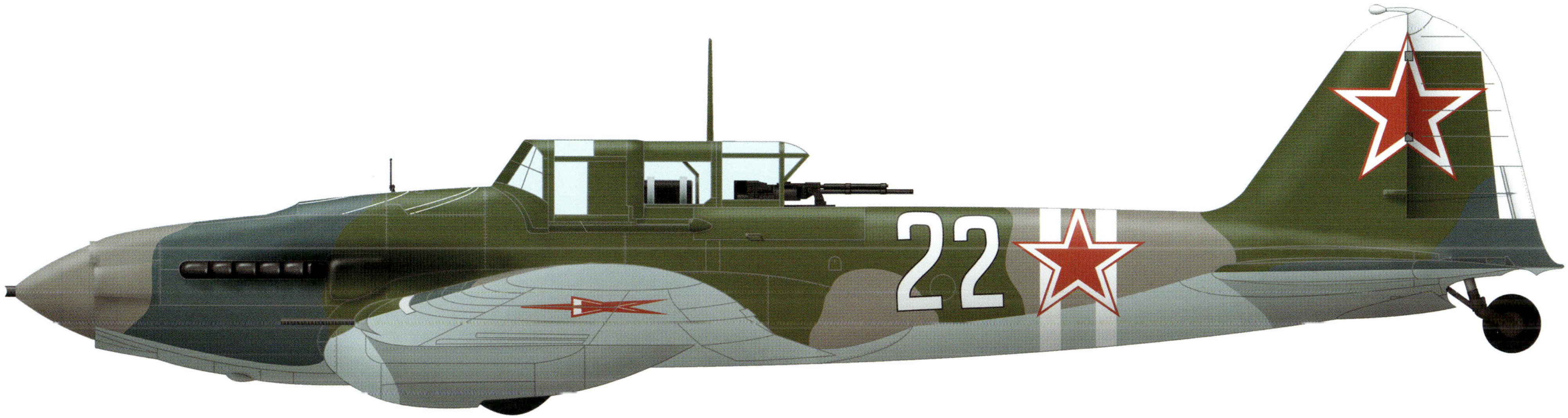

**Il-2 with swept wings, "white 22", 90th GShAP.**

**Flown by HSU Georgiy Timofeevich Beregovoy, later an astronaut taking part in the Soyuz 3 mission in 1968.**

Aircraft built in the Factory No.1 with wings of either wooden or metal construction. Standard camouflage pattern applied. Marking consists of standard red stars, tactical number, white bands on the fuselage and white areas on the tail. Some sources refer to the red nose but this marking feature is not clearly confirmed.

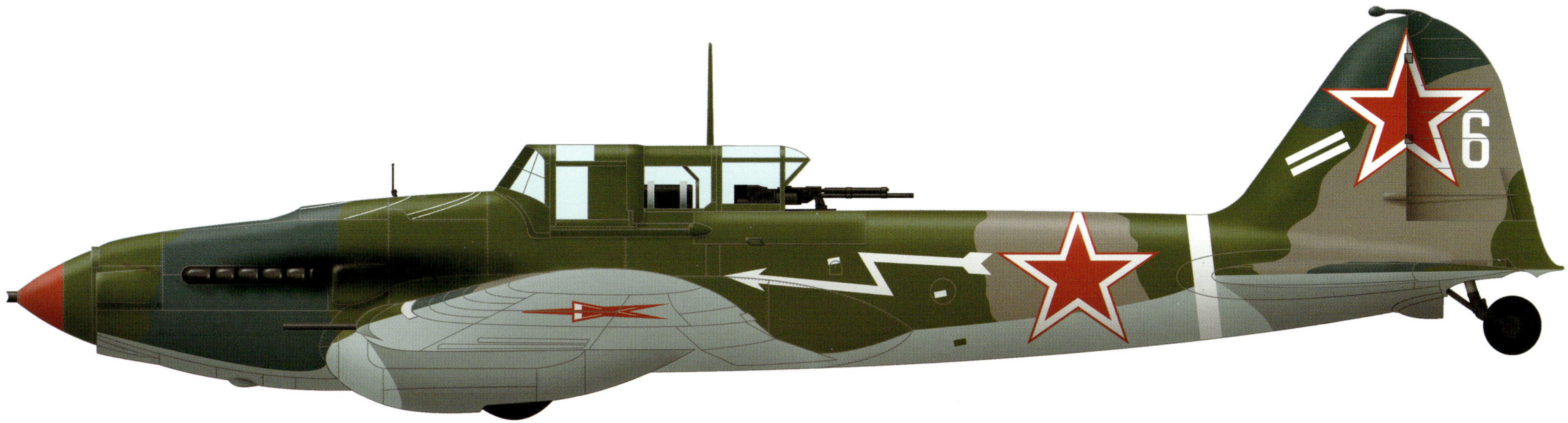


**Il-2 with swept wings, "white 6", 144$^{th}$ GShAP.**

**Unknown unit and location.**

Aircraft most likely built in the Factory No.18. That would indicate metal wings and possibly streamlined VYa-23 fairings. The standard camouflage pattern is a little bit modified on the vertical tail. The "white 6" shows an interesting identification marking.

## Il-2 with swept wings, "yellow 35".

### Unknown unit and location.

Aircraft built in the Factory No.1 with wings of either wooden or metal construction. Gunner's hinged canopy was removed. Standard camouflage pattern applied. Marking consists of standard red stars, white diagonal stripe on the vertical tail, probably yellow tactical number and red spinner tip.

## Il-2 “white 63”.

### Unknown unit and location.

Aircraft built in Factory No.18. Wings of metal construction with VYa-23 guns mounted. Canopy of early type with short antenna mast. Upper surfaces in green AMT-4 and black AMT-6. Undersides in light blue AMT-7. Marking consists of red stars with white outlines and white tactical number on the fuselage. The absence of the fuselage star is unusual.

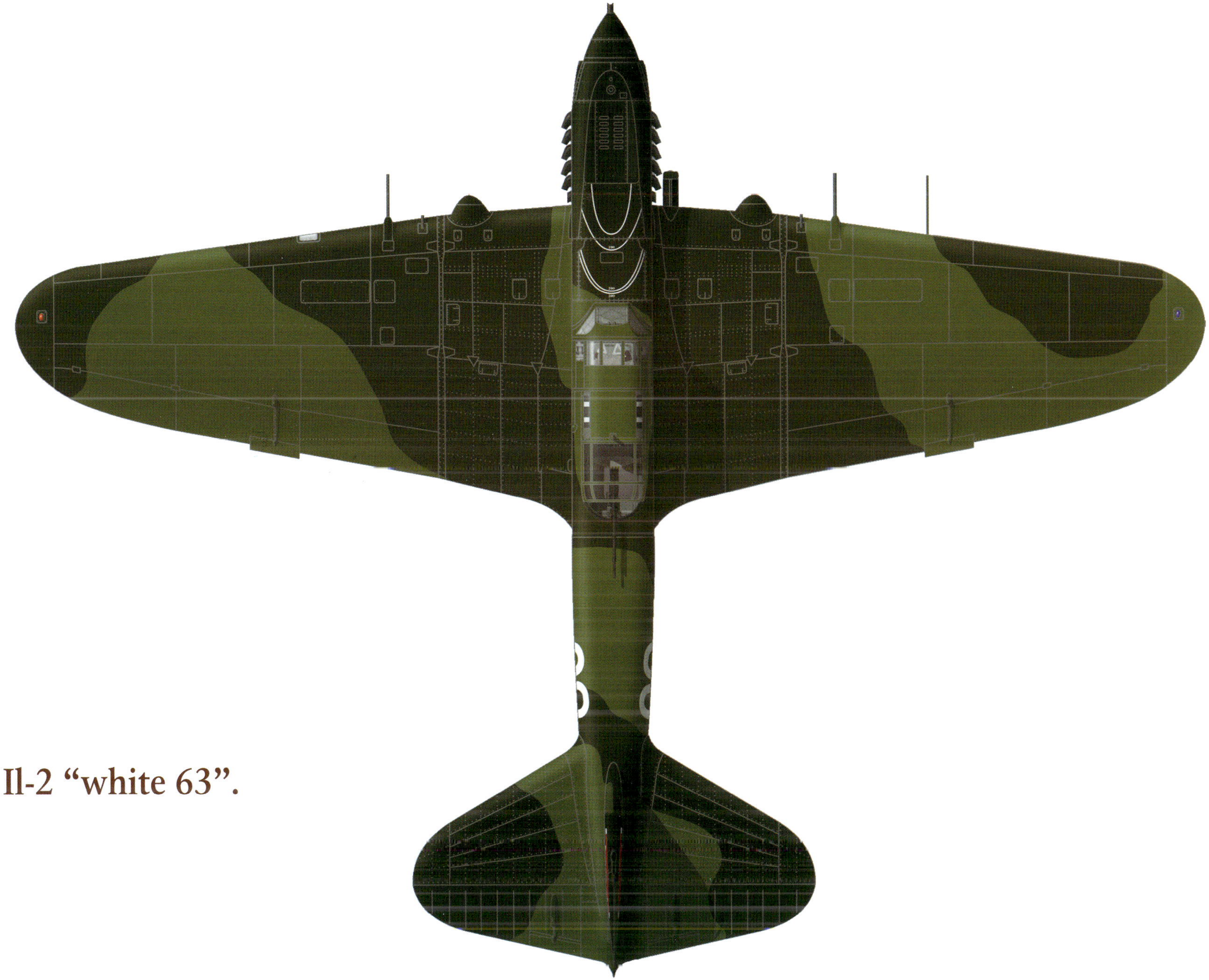

Il-2 “white 63”.

30

## Il-2 “white 75”.

### Unknown unit and location.

Early production aircraft fitted with wings of wooden construction with ShVAK guns mounted. Canopy of early type. Upper surfaces in green AMT-4 and black AMT-6. Undersides in light blue AMT-7. Marking consists of red stars and white tactical number on the fuselage.

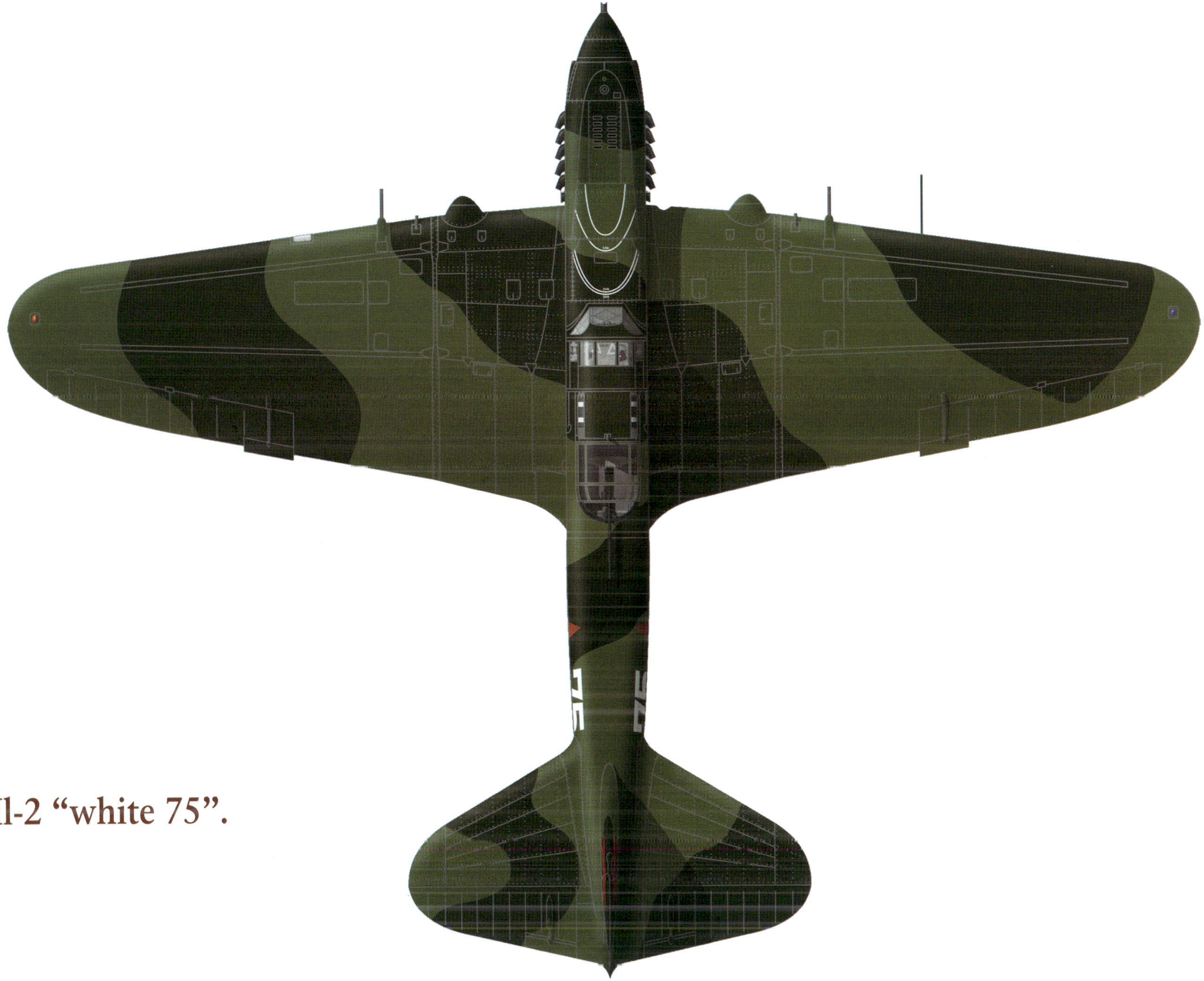

Il-2 “white 75”.

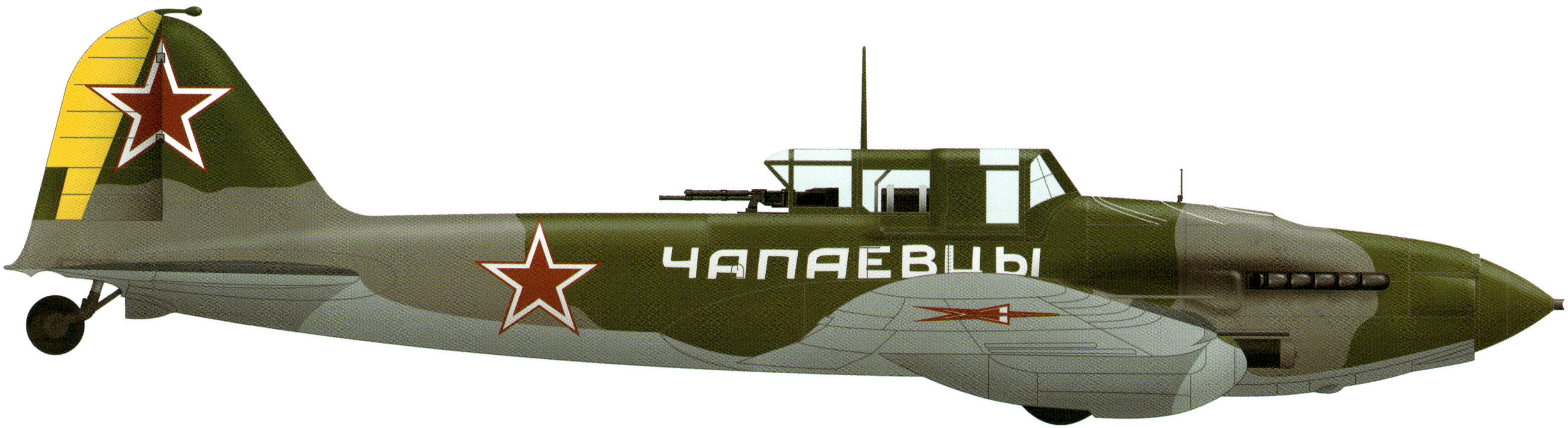


**Il-2 with swept wings "Chapayevtsi".**
**Unknown unit and location, spring 1945.**
This aircraft is one of thirteen Il-2s donated by citizens of Chapayenok, a town near the city of Kuybishev. Wings of metal construction.
Standard 1943 camouflage pattern applied. Marking consists of red stars with white and red outlines, white inscription on the fuselage and yellow area on the rudder.

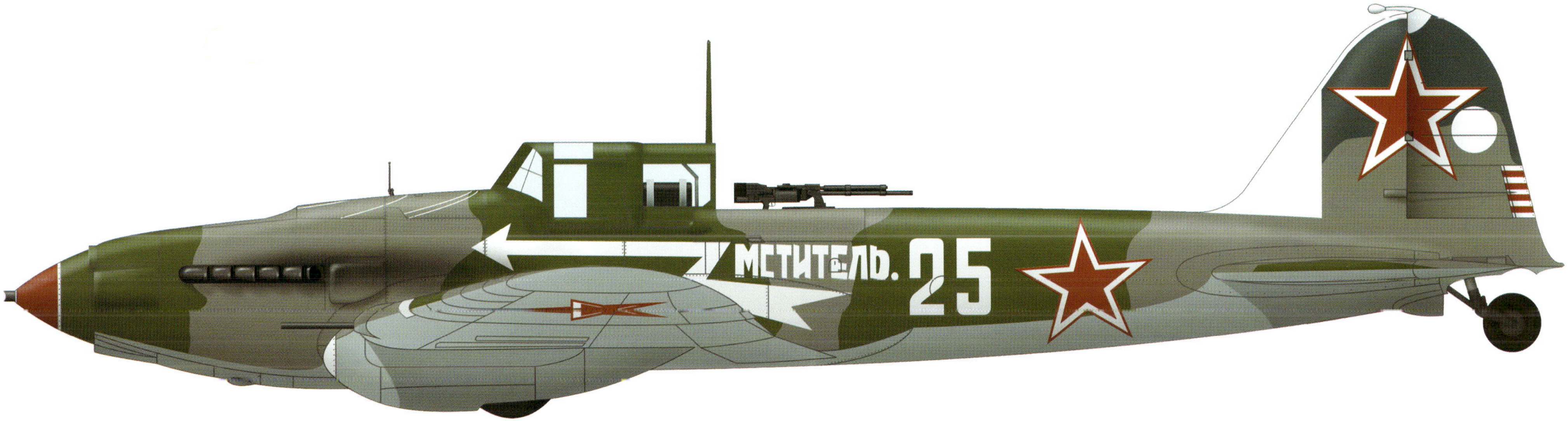


## Il-2 with swept wings "white 25" 567th ShAP, 198th ShAD, 16th VA.

**Berlin area, April 1945.**

Standard 1943 camouflage pattern applied. Marking is very interesting. Red stars with white and red outlines are completed with white tactical number, inscription and flash on the fuselage. On the tail, a large area was painted in white as well as fin leading edge. A white ball was added on the rudder. Trim tab is decorated with five white and four red stripes. Propeller spinner tip is red with thin white line. Also the main landing gear nacelle tips are painted in white. The inscription reads "Avenger".

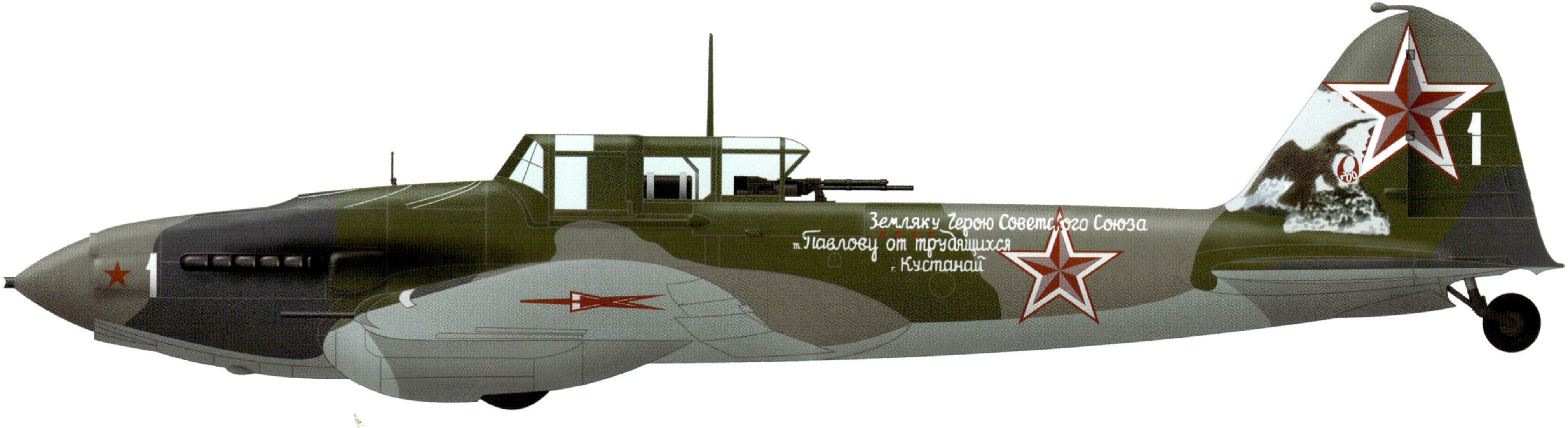


## Il-2 with swept wings "white 1", 6$^{th}$ GShAP, 1$^{st}$ Baltic Front, 3$^{rd}$ VA.

**Baltic area, autumn 1944 – spring 1945. Pilot Cpt. I. F. Pavlov awarded the title of HSU on 23$^{rd}$ February 1945.**

In April 1945, he took part in the Königsberg operation. Standard 1943 camouflage pattern applied. Marking is very interesting. Red stars of Kremlin style were completed with white tactical number applied on both rudder and nose. Small red star was painted on the nose as well. On the tail fin, a very elaborate drawing of an eagle was applied. The inscription on the fuselage, "Zemlyaku Geroyu Sovetskogo Soyuza t. Pavlovu ot Trudyashchikhsya g. Kustanay", reads "To the countryman Hero of the Soviet Union comrade Pavlov from the workers of the town of Kustanay". Additionally, four small red stars represent aerial victories achieved.

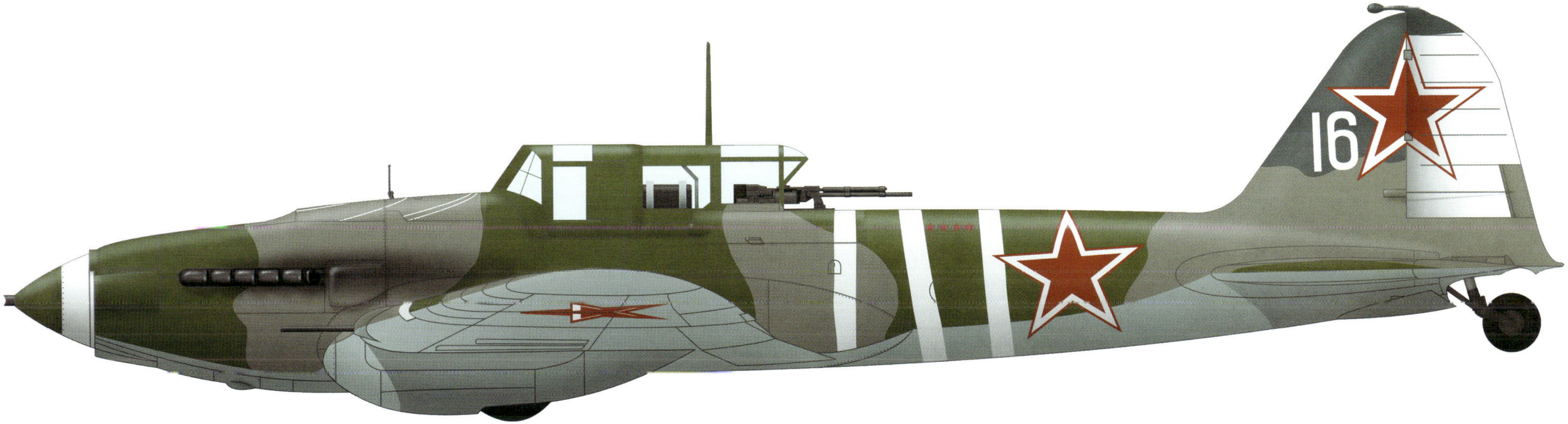


**Il-2 with swept wings "white 16".**

**Unknown unit and location.**

Standard 1943 camouflage pattern applied. Marking consists of red stars with white and red outlines, white tactical number, white rudder area, three white bands on the fuselage, white propeller spinner rear part and four small red stars representing achieved aerial kills.

**Il-2T "yellow 23", 23rd OShAP.**
**Black Sea Fleet, 1944.**
This drawing represents just a possible appearance.

37

## Il-2KR "white 482".

### Unknown unit and location.

Aircraft of late production with straight wings. The standard 1943 patterns is slightly modified with additional fields of dark grey color. Marking consists of red stars with white and red outlines. White tactical number is applied on the fuselage.

**Il-2 "white 71", 90th GShAP.**
**Unknown location.**

Late production aircraft with straight wings built in Factory No.1. Some aerodynamics improvement were applied, such as modified canopy, enlarged antenna mast, repositioned Pitot tube and enlarged tail landing gear fairing, which is typical for late Factory No.1 production. Standard 1943 pattern applied. Marking consists of red stars with white outlines, white vertical tail tip, white tactical number and two white fuselage bands.

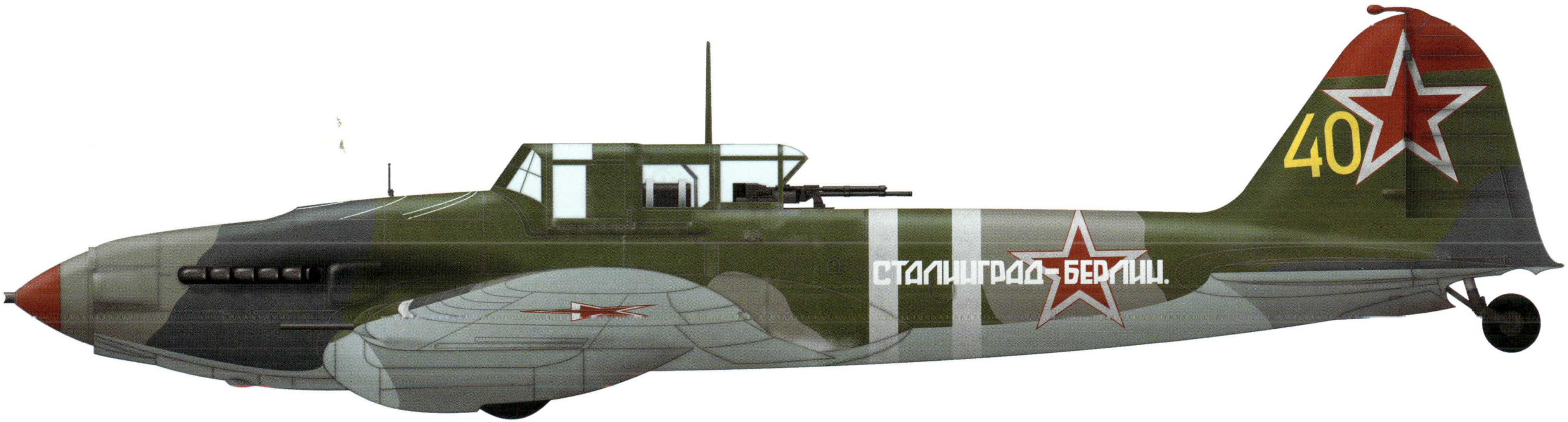


## Il-2 with swept wings "yellow 40", 56th GShAP.

### Unknown location.

In 1945, after the war, 56th GShAP participated in the movie called Victory. For this purpose, aircraft were decorated with the STALINGRAD–BERLIN inscription on both fuselage sides. The fresh white of the inscription was in contrast with worn white of the fuselage bands and red stars outlines.

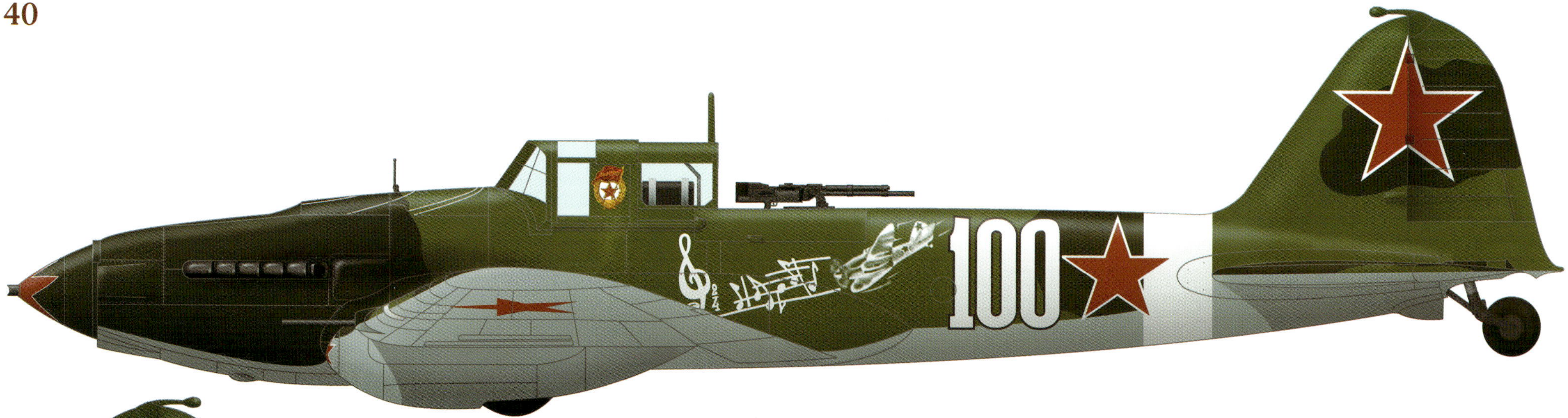

## Il-2 "white 100", 7th GShAP, 230th AD.

**August 1943. Pilot Capt. V. B. Emelyanenko, HSU, was the Moscow Academy of music student.**

Aircraft was built in Factory No.18. The gunner´s hinged canopy was removed. Upper surfaces in green AMT-4 and black AMT-6. Undersides in light blue AMT-7. Marking consists of red stars with white outlines, white tactical number with black outlines and white fuselage band. The large and elaborate drawing on the fuselage reflects Emelyanenko´s passion for music. Smal red stars with white outlines were applied on the propeller spinner and main landing gear nacelle tips as well as the Guard unit badge on the sliding canopy.

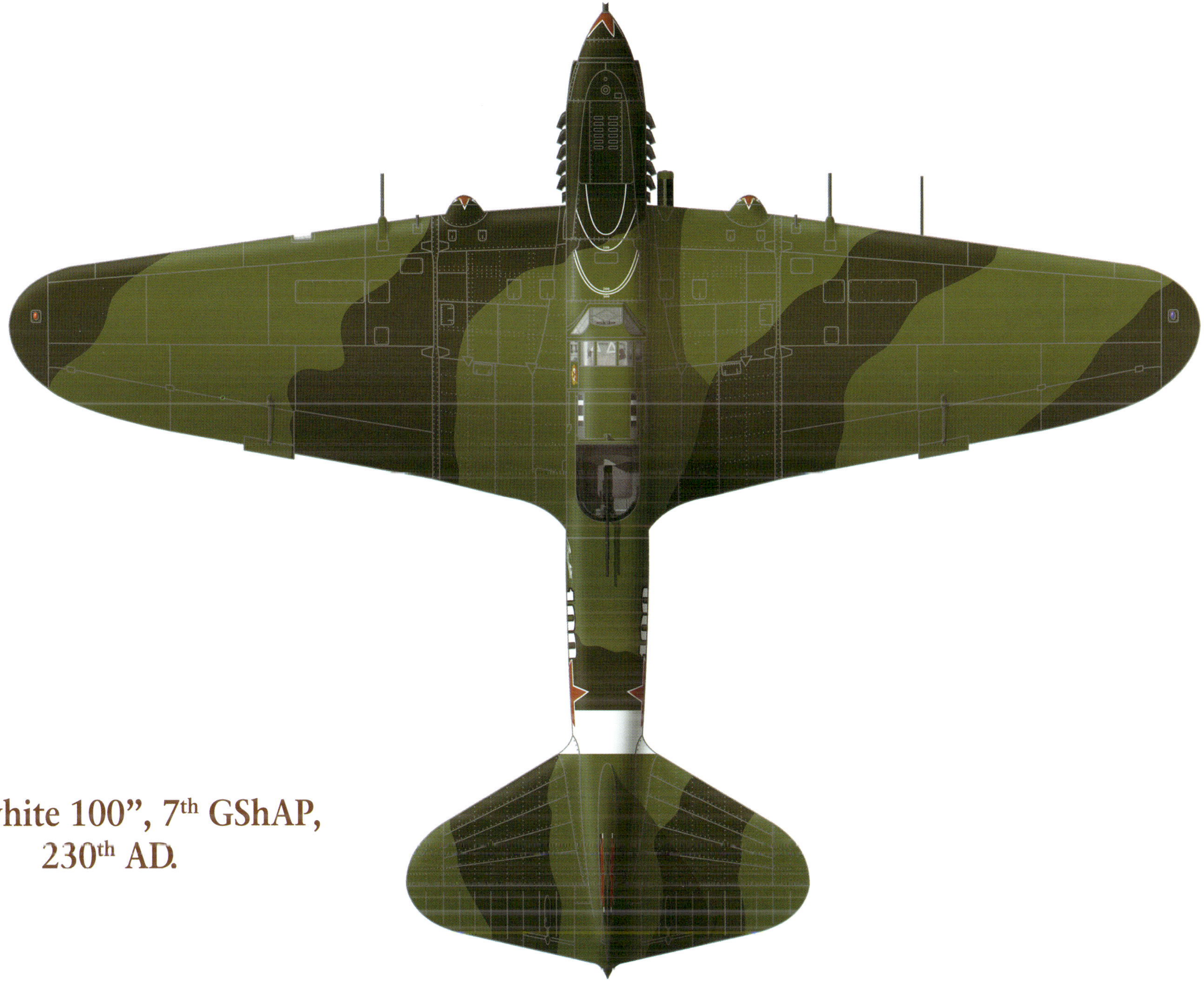

Il-2 “white 100”, 7th GShAP, 230th AD.

Published in Poland in 2020
by STRATUS sp.j.
Po. Box 123,
27-600 Sandomierz 1, Poland
e-mail: office@mmpbooks.biz
as
MMPBooks,

e-mail: office@mmpbooks.biz



**ISBN**
978-83-65958-68-6

*Editor in chief*
Roger Wallsgrove

*Editorial Team*
Bartłomiej Belcarz
Robert Pęczkowski
Artur Juszczak

*Colour profiles*
Viktor Povinsky

*DTP*
Stratus sp.j.

*Printed by*
Wydawnictwo Diecezjalne i Drukarnia w Sandomierzu
www.wds.pl

PRINTED IN POLAND

# Also in this series.

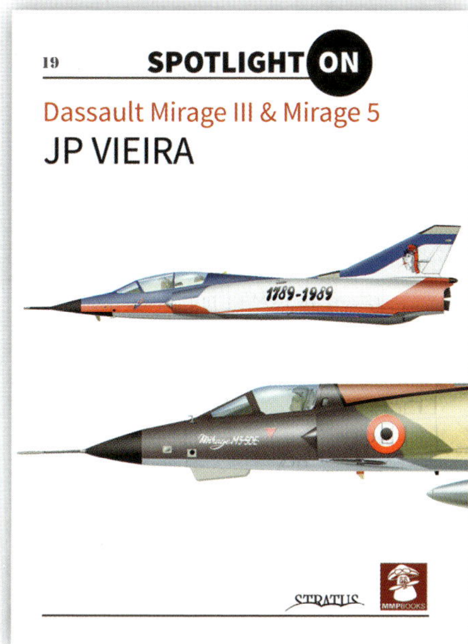